Junior Library of Money

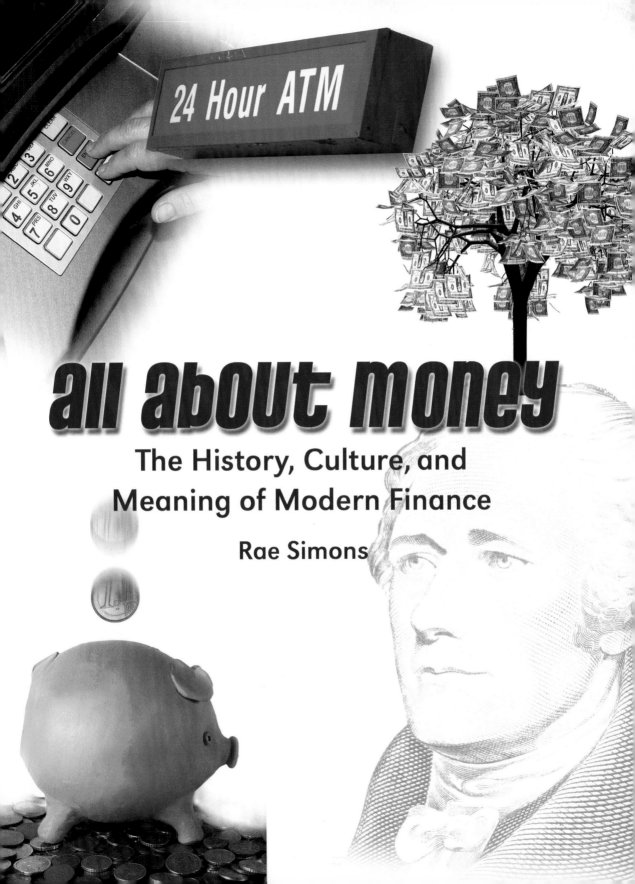

all about money

The History, Culture, and Meaning of Modern Finance

Rae Simons

MASON CREST PUBLISHERS INC.
370 Reed Road
Broomall, Pennsylvania 19008
(866)MCP-BOOK (toll free)
www.masoncrest.com

First Printing
9 8 7 6 5 4 3 2 1

Library of Congress Cataloging-in-Publication Data

Simons, Rae, 1957–
 All about money : the history, culture, and meaning of modern finance / by Rae Simons. – 1st ed.
     p. cm. — (Junior library of money)
 Includes bibliographical references and index.
 ISBN 978-1-4222-1760-3 (hbk.)   ISBN 978-1-4222-1759-7 (series)
 ISBN 978-1-4222-1879-2 (pbk.)   ISBN 978-1-4222-1878-5 (pbk. series)
 1. Money—Juvenile literature. I. Title.
 HG221.5.S56 2011
 332.4'9—dc22
                              2010021818

Design by Wendy Arakawa.
Produced by Harding House Publishing Service, Inc.
www.hardinghousepages.com
Cover design by Torque Advertising and Design.
Printed by Bang Printing.

CONTENT$

Introduction

Our lives interact with the global financial system on an almost daily basis: we take money out of an ATM machine, we use a credit card to go shopping at the mall, we write a check to pay the rent, we apply for a loan to buy a new car, we set something aside in a savings account, we hear on the evening news whether the stock market went up or down. These interactions are not just frequent, they are consequential. Deciding whether to attend college, buying a house, or saving enough for retirement, are decisions with large financial implications for almost every household. Even small decisions like using a debit or a credit card become large when made repeatedly over time.

And yet, many people do not understand how to make good financial decisions. They do not understand how inflation works or why it matters. They do not understand the long-run costs of using consumer credit. They do not understand how to assess whether attending college makes sense, or whether or how much money they should borrow to do so. They do not understand the many different ways there are to save and invest their money and which investments make the most sense for them.

And because they do not understand, they make mistakes. They run up balances they cannot afford to repay on their credit card. They drop out of high school and end up unemployed or trying to make ends meet on a minimum wage job, or they borrow so much to pay for college that they are drowning in debt when they graduate. They don't save enough. They pay high interests rates and fees when lower cost options are available. They don't buy insurance to protect themselves from financial risks. They find themselves declaring bankruptcy, with their homes in foreclosure.

We can do better. We must do better. In an increasingly sophisticated financial world, everyone needs a basic knowledge of our financial system. The books in this series provide

just such a foundation. The series has individual books devoted specifically to the financial decisions most relevant to children: work, school, and spending money. Other books in the series introduce students to the key institutions of our financial system: money, banks, the stock market, the Federal Reserve, the FDIC. Collectively they teach basic financial concepts: inflation, interest rates, compounding, risk vs. reward, credit ratings, stock ownership, capitalism. They explain how basic financial transactions work: how to write a check, how to balance a checking account, what it means to borrow money. And they provide a brief history of our financial system, tracing how we got where we are today.

There are benefits to all of us of having today's children more financially literate. First, if we can help the students of today start making wise financial choices when they are young, they can hopefully avoid the financial mishaps that have been so much in the news of late. Second, as the financial crisis of 2007–2010 has shown, poor individual financial choices can sometimes have implications for the health of the overall financial system, something that affects everyone. Finally, the financial system is an important part of our overall economy. The students of today are the business and political leaders of tomorrow. We need financially literate citizens to choose the leaders who will guide our economy through the inevitable changes that lie ahead.

Brigitte Madrian, Ph.D.
Aetna Professor of Public Policy
and Corporate Management
Harvard Kennedy School

What Is Money?

You learned about money when you were still little. Before you were very old, you had discovered that these pieces of green paper and round metal discs could be exchanged for the things you wanted. You learned that four quarters made a dollar, that pennies were bigger than dimes and yet not worth as much, and that George Washington's face was on a dollar bill. You saved up change and Grandma's Christmas gifts in your piggy bank. Maybe you even had your own bank account. You looked forward to going to the store and spending your money.

But have you ever thought about what money really IS?

Long ago, people traded with each other, one thing for another. For instance, suppose one farmer grew pumpkins and another raised cows. The one farmer might trade a pumpkin for a bucket of milk. Or he might trade a whole field, good for growing pumpkins, in exchange for five cows.

You might do something similar. Suppose your friend has a computer game you want—and your friend wants your bike. You decide that the bike and the computer game are worth about the same to each of you, and you agree to trade. No money has been exchanged, and yet you both have ended up with what you wanted.

But you can't walk into a store at the mall pushing your bicycle—or carrying a pumpkin—and offer to exchange it for some new jewelry. Money fits into your pocket a lot easier than a pumpkin!

Money is something our world has agreed to use as a symbol for the things we value. It's not really the magic thing you may have thought it was when you were little. In a way, it stands for the same thing a pump-kin or a cow does—something someone worked hard to produce that is of value to others as well.

The History of Money

Barter

Barter is the word that describes exchanging one type of goods for another—a bicycle for a computer game, for instance.

For hundreds of years, barter was the main way many people did business. People brought their goods to a central marketplace once a week, where they could display what they

had to trade and see what everyone else had. Sometimes, even in our own country as recently as a hundred years ago, people might trade food for a service. For instance, a doctor or a lawyer might be paid with a chicken or a bag of grain.

In some places in the world, people still barter. The South American marketplace shown above, for example, is a place where people can trade goods with each other, just like the **medieval** market shown on the opposite page. Some people may use money, but many will not.

You may think that trading a bag of onions for six ears of corn doesn't sound like a very interesting purchase. But if you lived in a simpler world, the main things you would need would be food and clothing. You wouldn't need computer games or iPods or new bicycles. Instead, you and your family would work hard to raise certain crops. These would be the things of value you would have to offer, and you would trade them for things that other people had made or grown. Sometimes you might trade skills and services: you might, for example, build a new roof for someone in exchange for some new clothes.

As long as life is simple, the barter system works. But when life becomes more complicated, people need a new system for exchanging wealth.

Cattle, Corn, and Cowrie

In most places in the world, cattle were the earliest **currency**. Remember Jack, who took his cow to the market, but traded it along the way for a magic bean? His mother was angry with him for spending his cow foolishly, the way your mother might be angry if you spent all your allowance on candy.

Grain—what was called "corn" in England, though it wasn't the corn we know today—was another early form of currency. A bag of grain had an agreed-upon value that could purchase other goods and services.

In some parts of the world, including Africa, Asia, and the Pacific Islands, cowrie shells were the currency for hundreds of years. Even after money began to be used, people in Africa, for instance, could still exchange 2,000 cowries for one dollar. Different kinds of shells were used instead of money in other parts of the world. In North America, the native people used clam shells to create "wampum," which they used for currency, exchanging the shell beads for the things they wanted. Shells were a lot more convenient and portable than either a cow or a bag of grain!

The First Coins

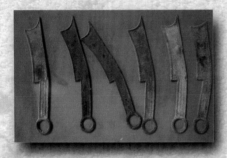

In China, the first coins were actually metal cowrie shells. These were then replaced with metal ceremonial knives and spades that were used as money. They began to be used about 600 BCE. Some of these looked like the blades and spades shown to the left on this page, while others were the jagged shapes shown on the opposite page.

Eventually, about 250 BCE, the Chinese began using round coins that could be strung together through a center hole, as shown in the bottom right corner of the opposite page.

Meanwhile, coins that look more familiar to us today began to be made around 300 BCE in both Rome and Greece. For the first time, people's faces and writing appeared on coins.

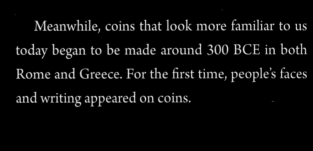

The ancient people of India were also creating their own coins at about the same time that China and Asia Minor (modern-day Turkey) came up with the idea. The government of India started creating its own coins in about 600 BCE. Like other early coins—and the coins we still use today—these small pieces of metal bore an official stamp to prove that their weight and value had been approved by government authority.

This was one of the earliest coins ever made, from Lydia, a city in what is now Turkey. During the years around 600 BCE, it was worth about 11 goats or 9 jars of wine.

Coins spread from Asia Minor (modern-day Turkey) to ancient Greece and Rome.

A coin is a piece of metal with a standardized weight (in other words, each coin weighs the same as any other coin).

DID YOU KNOW?

It is produced in large quantities, and it also has a standardized value. There's nothing that says it has to be round!

During the time these coins were used in China, a person could earn about 2,000 during a month. A horse was worth about 4,500, and a bag of rice could be bought with 140 coins.

BANKNOTES

The earliest banknotes—the forerunners of our modern-day paper bills—were basically I.O.U.s written on pieces of paper. They were notes people had written that promised to

pay a certain amount of metal coinage. Often, notes were based on the value of grain and cattle. So someone might write a note to someone else, promising to pay them a certain amount of grain or a certain number of cows.

The first official paper money was made in China. Carrying around strings of coins (like the ones shown on page 15) could get to be awkward; the coins were heavy and bulky. To solve this problem, coins were often left with a trustworthy person, and the merchant was given a slip of paper recording how much money he had left with that person. When he brought the paper back, he could regain his money.

Around 900 CE, paper money like that shown to the left began to be offically issued in China for use throughout the country.

In Europe, the first paper money was issued in 1574 in Leyden, a city in what is today the Netherlands, when it was under seige during a war with Spain. Cut off from the rest of the world, there was no metal available for coinage; even leather (which was often used to create emergency cur-rency) had been

boiled and used to feed the people. So to create currency, the residents took paper from hymnals and church missals and created paper money. The first official banknotes, however, would not be issued in Europe until nearly a hundred years later.

In North America, in the early 1690s, the Massachusetts Bay Colony was the first to issue permanently **circulating** banknotes. The use of fixed **denominations** and printed banknotes came into use in the 1700s when each of the thirteen colonies issued their own. During the Revolutionary War, the Continental Congress issued paper currency to pay for the war, but the U.S. federal government did not print banknotes until 1862.

Have you ever heard the expression "to pay through the nose"? It's a phrase that means to pay a lot for something. Historians think the saying began

DID YOU KNOW?

when people in Britain who couldn't pay their taxes had their noses slit as punishment!

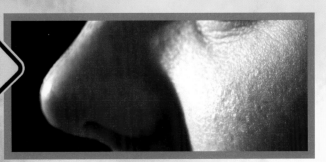

The Birth of American Money

The first paper money issued by the Massachusetts Bay Colony was used to pay soldiers returning from an expedition to Quebec. The notes promised the bearer that they could be **redeemed** in gold or silver. They could be used immediately to pay taxes and were accepted as legal **tender**. One of these notes is shown at the bottom of the next page.

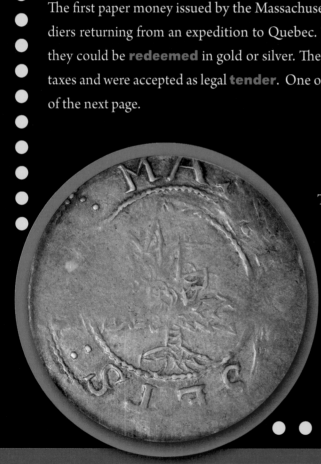

The first coins to circulate in the young United States were usually foreign coins from Spain, England, or France, but in 1792, the first U.S. **mint** began producing American coins.

Another early form of paper money used in North America was "tobacco notes" (shown above). These were certificates attesting to the quality and quantity of tobacco deposited in public warehouses. These certificates could be circulated much more conveniently than the actual tobacco leaves and were accepted as money throughout most of the 18th century.

Before the Revolutionary War, each of the colonies issued their own paper money. Sometimes, individual business-men would even create their own banknotes. After Congress adopted the Constitution in 1789, it chartered the First Bank of the United States. The bank was authorized to issue paper banknotes to reduce confusion and simplify trade.

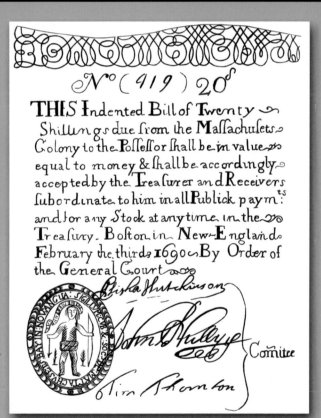

American Money in the Early 1800s

The First Bank of America was only chartered through 1811—and then the War of 1812 came along. When the war was over, the Second Bank of America was established, but President Andrew Jackson did not trust banks, and so he kept the federal bank from having any power to regulate money across the growing country. As a result, not only could each state issue their own paper money, but so could cities, groups of private individuals, even drug stores.

A "Free Banking" movement sprang up in America. Citizens claimed they had the right to set up banks rather than be dependent on seeking that privilege from the State. As a result, banks across America varied from **reputable**, trustworthy institutions to worthless "wild-catters" that profited from making quick note issues and then moving on.

The total number of banks in the United States rose from 330 in 1830 to a pre-Civil War peak of 1,601 in 1861. These banks poured out a flood of banknotes, most of which were accepted only at a discount from their face value.

Imagine how confusing it would be to do business if you had to use more than 1,500 different kinds of paper bills! Bankers and merchants had to constantly refer to one or other of a series of banknote guides. One of these guides, *Hodges Genuine Bank Notes of America*, published in 1859, listed 9,916 notes issued by 1,365 banks, and even then, hundreds of genuine banknotes had been left out.

The situation created a counterfeiter's paradise. With so many different kinds of bills circulating, it was very hard to tell which were genuine and which were fake. During the first half of the nineteenth century, as many as 5,400 different kinds of counterfeit notes were floating through Americans' wallets and bank accounts (despite the best efforts of the banks themselves, which had set up in 1853 the Association for the Prevention of Counterfeiting).

DID YOU KNOW?

Paper money used to be backed by gold. Each bill could technically be exchanged for its worth in gold (or silver). Today, however, our money (both coins and paper) is "fiat" money. It has no *intrinsic* value.

WAR AND MONEY

When the North and the South went to war during the American Civil War, both sides needed money to pay for the costs of battle. Both the American federal government and the South's Confederate government issued paper money. The South printed more bills than it had wealth, and the paper dollars soon became worthless, but the North did a better job handling currency at the national level.

Many politicians that had been against a strong central national bank had been from the South to start with. When the South dropped out of the Union, other politicians in the North had the chance to reform America's money system. In 1862, "Greenbacks" came into existence when the U.S. Treasury was given the right to issue notes that were authorized as legal tender.

The National Banking Act passed by Congress in 1863 allowed banks to be chartered by the U.S. Treasury. Banknotes were then printed by the U.S. Treasury using a standard design but with the bank's name, state, and charter number on the note. The notes were signed by U.S. Treasury officials like today, as well as by the bank's officials.

During the Civil War, people worried about their finances, and many people hoarded coins. This meant that there were not enough coins in ciculation, creating a greater need for paper money. The first U.S. paper notes were printed in denominations of 1 cent, 5 cents, 25 cents, and 50 cents. Later, larger denominations were made.

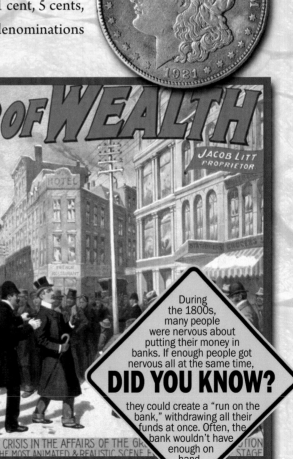

DID YOU KNOW?

During the 1800s, many people were nervous about putting their money in banks. If enough people got nervous all at the same time, they could create a "run on the bank," withdrawing all their funds at once. Often, the bank wouldn't have enough on hand.

MODERN MONEY

In the 20th century, there were six different kinds of United States bills:

- United States Notes
- Gold Certificates
- National Banknotes
- Silver Certificates
- Federal Reserve Banknotes
- Federal Reserve Notes

Each of these bills worked a little differently, but today, there is only one kind of paper money in America: Federal Reserve Notes. Today, all paper money is issued directly by the U.S. government.

The first bills came in large denominations that went up as high as 10,000 and even 100,000.

The motto "In God We Trust" has been on American coins since the Civil War, when there was a new surge of religious belief in America.

DID YOU KNOW?

"Our God and Our Country" was also proposed as a possible motto for American coins.

Today, however, these large bills have been discontinued. People use either checks or **electronic** money transfers for large amounts of money. Also, the War on Drugs that began in the 1980s discouraged the creation of large bills, since they could be used to make large purchases anonymously.

Two-dollar bills have been made at various times in the history of U.S. bills, but they've never caught on. For some reason, people don't trust them. They like to collect them, but they also seem to think they're not REAL money. Or they think they're bad luck!

DID YOU KNOW?

The dollar sign has been used since the 1770s. It was originally an abbreviation for the Spanish peso—a P with an S. The two letters came to be written on top of each other, and Americans adopted it for use with dollars.

Money Around the World

Each country around the world has its own currency, with its own unit of money.

In Europe, many countries share a common currency—the euro. Because people travel easily between countries in Europe, their economies are hard to separate from one another. So many European countries got together and formed the European Union, agreeing to share a common currency. The new euro comes in both coins and paper money. Euro banknotes look the same in all the countries, but euro coins have different designs on the backs, depending on which country made it. Some European countries did not adopt the euro. Great Britain, Sweden, and Denmark like having their own national currencies and plan to keep on using them.

Most of the rest of the world also uses their own national currencies. Most businesses do not accept foreign money, and each nation's unit of money has a different value compared to other nation's money. That value changes, at least slightly, every day. People in other countries need to exchange money at a bank or at a currency exchange.

The Spanish peso—what was then known as "pieces of eight"—was once the **standard** for world currency, and almost any nation would accept Spanish gold coins. Today, the dollar is the world's standard. Some small countries do not even bother to make their own money and simply use U.S. dollars. Other countries, however, are beginning to use the euro as their standard instead of the dollar.

What Does Money Look

Australia (Dollar)

Brazil (Real)

Denmark (Krone)

Ethiopia (Birr)

Ghana (Cedi)

Haiti (Gourde)

India (Rupee)

Iraq (Dinar)

Isreal (Lirot)

Like Around the World?

Mexico (Peso)

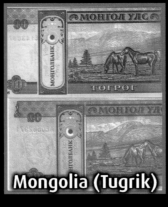

Mongolia (Tugrik)

Romania (Lei)

Russia (Ruble)

South Korea (Won)

Suriname (Gulden)

Switzerland (Franc)

Thailand (Bhat)

Viet Nam (Dong)

Electronic Money

In today's modern world, it's not always necessary to use currency at all. Much money exists electronically, in the memory banks of computers. This means that nowadays, when you make a deposit in a bank, many times no bills or coins are involved in the transaction.

Say you have an after-school job at the local grocery store. You get your paycheck on Friday and take it to the bank to deposit it in your checking account. There's no little guy running money bags between the two banks, and nothing even goes through the mail. Instead, funds from the grocery store's bank are moved electronically to your bank. You now have access to that money. If you want, you can use it to buy a song off the Internet; in which case, again, an electronic transfer of funds will be made, this time from your bank account to someone else's. The electronic money can continue on like this indefinitely, going from account to account without any actual bills or coins being exchanged.

You might start to wonder what money really IS then, if these days, it isn't cows or cowries . . . it isn't silver or gold . . . and it isn't even dollars and cents, at least not the kind you can hold in your hand. But what hasn't changed is that money is a way to measure what we value. That might be time and effort (your time and effort at the grocery store, for example)—or it might be an object like a car—or it might be a song from the Internet.

Of course, you can still stop the flow of electronic money any time you want and change it into the kind of money you can put into your wallet. Just go to an ATM, insert your bank card, punch in your password—and the machine will convert your electronic funds into bills it spits out into your hand!

THE FUTURE OF MONEY

But will we always be able to change electronic money into currency, the bills and coins with which we are so familiar today? Will we even NEED to?

Some financial experts say that digital money will be the currency of the future, dollars and cents that exist only in the world's electronic computer network. Some systems of electronic money already exist.

Technically, digital money is a representation, a system of debits and credits, used to exchange value. There are several such systems, including Paypal, Gogopay, WebMoney, and others. Some cities, such as Hong Kong, have a system of electronic money; Hong Kong's is called the Octopus Card. The Octopus Card started out as a system of payment for public transportation, and then grew to include other money transactions. Singapore and the Netherlands are developing similar systems as well.

Although digital cash can provide many benefits—such as convenience and privacy, increased efficiency of transactions, lower **transaction** fees, and new business opportunities with the expansion of Internet business—digital cash also involves new dangers and challenges. If all money transactions take place on the Internet, governments will have a hard time regulating what goes on. How do governments make sure taxes are paid, for example? How do they keep "money" tied to something in the real world, instead of it becoming a purely imaginary concept that can be created electronically? Money and crime have always gone hand in hand, but electronic money offers opportunities to a whole new type of bad guy—the **cyber** criminal. **Laundering** money could become much easier if all money exists only on the Internet and can't be traced back to its source. Bank robberies become a matter of changing a database in the banks' computers. These challenges will mean that new regulations will need to be passed to monitor the world of electronic money.

WHAT IS THE ECONOMY?

When people talk about the economy, they are referring to everything that has to do with the production and distribution of goods and services within a country. This means all the jobs that people have, all the things they make and grow, all the services they provide, all the things they buy and sell, the natural resources they have available (such as oil or trees or precious metals), and the system of money they use—all these things are parts of the economy. As long as people have been making and distributing goods or services, there has been some sort of economy. The early economies were far simpler (and easier to understand!). Economies grew larger as societies grew and became more complex.

The best way to understand the U.S. economy is by looking at Gross Domestic Product (GDP). This is the **statistic** economists (specialists who study the economy) use to measure the economy. The U.S. economy, as measured by GDP, is everything produced by all the people and all the companies in the United States.

Despite all the problems America has with its economy, it is still one of the richest nations in the world, with one of the highest GDPs.

The map on the next page shows the GDPs of all the nations of the world.

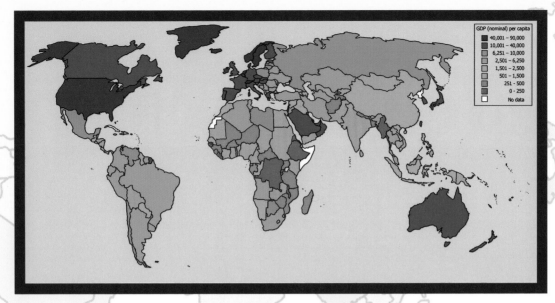

Dark blue = the richest nations of the world.

At the time this map was created in 2000, the richest nations included the United States and some of the European nations, such as Norway, Sweden, Denmark, and the Netherlands. Next in line are the nations colored lighter blue on this map, including Canada and Australia, as well as much of Europe. The very poorest countries of the world—the ones with the lowest GDPs and the least successful economies—are colored red on this map. They include some of the nations in Africa and Asia. However, economies are constantly changing, and China's GDP has increased to the point that it is now at the second level.

So what does all this mean for human beings? Most of the people who live in countries with higher GDPs have better standards of living. In other words, they can purchase the services and goods they need to be healthy and happy. Meanwhile, most of the people who live in countries with lower GDPs also have lower standards of living. Of course, very rich people can live in very poor countries, and very poor people can live in rich nations. Economy touches the lives of all the individuals in a particular region, but it is a word that refers to the big picture of entire regions, not the small picture of individuals.

THE GLOBAL ECONOMY

More and more, in today's world, the economies of the Earth's different nations affect each other. Countries have traded with each other for thousands of years, of course, but in the past twenty years or so, the process known as "globalization" has begun to move much more quickly. There are several reasons for this.

First, corporations often do business across borders. For example, Japanese car companies have factories in the United States—and their cars are sold all around the world. American companies like Nike also have factories in nations around the world, and the goods they produce—sneakers and sportswear—are sold everywhere.

Another factor that's contributing to the growth of a global economy is the ease with which people and goods can move across boundary lines, from nation to nation. This is the result of treaties between governments, encouraging the flow of both goods and people between nations.

New forms of communication and technology have also speeded up the process of globalization. In the days when Americans had no idea what was happening in China—and vice versa—until weeks later, few Americans felt that events in China had much bearing on their lives. Today, however, we can see events around the world instantly on our televisions and computers. Businesspeople and investors can also respond immediately, taking advantage of new opportunities.

Last, and perhaps most important, the Internet has connected the planet in new ways. Not only can we communicate with each other but we can also provide services to each other, around the globe. This means workers in India can work for American companies. A craftsperson in American can sell her creations to people in Russia.

Money and Culture

Money makes the world go round.

Money means many things (it's a complicated topic!), but for thousands of years, it's played an important role in human cultures. Think of all the wise sayings that have to do with money!

A penny saved is a penny earned.

Money is the root of all evil.

Money talks.

How you doing?

ONE DOLLAR

Do you know what each of these sayings means? Can you think of any others?

Money doesn't grow on trees.

Americans
& Wealth

$

Some of the very first Europeans who came to North America came here because they were hoping to get rich. Even those who came to pursue religious freedom were also looking for opportunities to support themselves and their families. These early Americans worked hard. They created a new kind of society where it was possible to begin life poor and end up rich, instead of being trapped in the class to which your parents had belonged before you.

"The American Dream" was the term people used for this idea—the concept that everyone in the United States was entitled to the same opportunities to accumulate wealth. Of course, the American Dream wasn't completely true: if you were a woman in 1950, for instance, you didn't have the same opportunities for accumulating wealth that a man did during that same era. And if you were a black man in the early 20th century, you were a lot less likely to become wealthy than if you were a white man. Still, it was a *dream*, a dream that inspired many people to do great things.

America values freedom and democracy—the ability to shape our government and our laws—and Americans have always connected these values with the opportunity to be prosperous (to become wealthy, in other words). "Capitalism" is the word that describes America's economic systems, or "free enterprise"—a system where the government allows private companies to run the economy, allowing the forces of supply and demand to shape the way business takes place, while private individuals and companies accumulate as much wealth as they can.

When the American Dream seems impossible to achieve, many Americans become disillusioned and angry with their government. Despite the ups and downs of the economy, however, material wealth—money—is as important to Americans as ever. They love television shows that create games or "reality" scenarios where contestants can get rich quick. They worry about money. They dream of winning the lottery. America has a love affair with money!

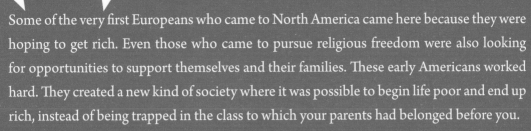

In the early days of America, the "American Dream" had more to do with the land that was available, especially as the nation moved West.

DID YOU KNOW?

In the 20th century, the "American Dream" often referred to owning your own house. And today it has to do with education and jobs.

The History of Capitalism

The earliest roots of capitalism can be found thousands of years ago, during the Roman Empire (or even earlier), when merchants who sailed the Mediterranean Sea accumulated wealth from their business dealings. Unlike today, there were no great factories or industries producing wealth. Instead, these wealthy merchants (shown doing their business in the image to the right) acted as go-betweens between farmers, miners, and craftspeople, getting rich from the web of trade they created.

In the 1770s, an Englishman named Adam Smith developed the theory that became the foundation for modern-day capitalism. Smith said that if government stayed out of the marketplace, allowing individuals to be motivated by the chance of earning more money, business would prosper. He believed that in the long run, the free exchange of goods would

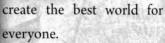

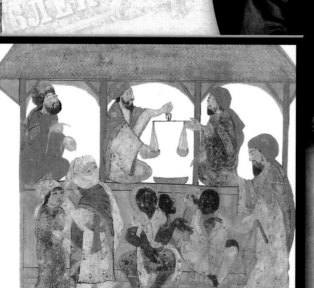

create the best world for everyone.

Adam Smith's capitalism was an outgrowth of the Enlightenment, the movement begun by philosophers like Voltaire (shown above). The **philosophy** of the Enlightenment focused on the rights of the individual; it defined progress as endless economic growth. It was the same philosophy that helped spark the American Revolution, so it's no wonder that capitalism and democracy are firmly linked in many Americans' minds! Individual freedom and the right to accumulate wealth without government interference are basic to Americans' thinking.

Modern Capitalism

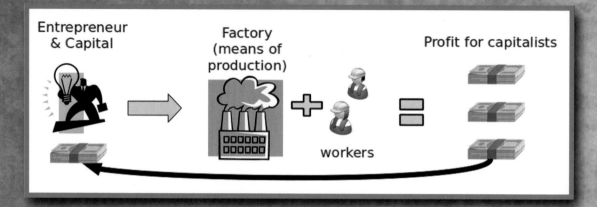

The Industrial Revolution changed the way capitalism worked. With the growth of factories, goods could now be produced in large quantities. Typically, an entrepreneur—a person with money and ideas—would create a factory (or many factories) to produce lots of some good that people wanted (for example, cloth). The factory would hire workers (lots of workers) to make the product (in this case cloth), and the owner of the company would then sell the cloth (or whatever) to other businesspeople who would eventually turn around and sell the goods to consumers (ordinary people who needed clothing, for instance).

In order for the business owner to make a profit, he needed to spend less money on creating the product than he got from the people who bought his product.

This meant that money would keep coming back to him, and he would get rich. The workers in his factory, however, did not get to share in the owner's profits, and they did not usually get rich.

However, capitalism looks at the big picture. It says that a system like this, where people have the freedom to accumulate as much wealth as they can, will in the long run be good for everyone. Businesses will thrive, creating more jobs—and more jobs mean more consumers (more people who have money to buy the goods), which will make the businesses grow even more, making still more jobs, and so on and so on.

Capitalism is an economic system, but it is also linked in Americans' minds with their political system (the way the country is governed). Today, not all Americans feel that capitalism and democracy need to go hand-in-hand, and other nations have experimented with other economic systems. Most Americans remain loyal to capitalism; however, the system upon which America was built.

Money and the Meaning of Life

We've come a long way from cows to capitalism! And yet since the very earliest cultures (the ones that used cows instead of coins), money (or wealth) has always been mixed up with the meaning of life.

What do you think are the most important things in life? Land? Houses and cars? Or lots and lots of THINGS, the many, many items that fill our malls and shopping centers?

It can get very confusing! We live in a world where consuming—buying the stuff that's for sale in stores—is an essential part of what keeps our world's economy healthy. Shopping is a part of all our lives. It's difficult to imagine life being any other way.

But life wasn't always like this. People used to make the things they needed. Or they personally knew the people who DID make those things. The world was simpler then. It was easier to see the connections between people, and to understand how things affected everybody within a particular economy, from the people who grew the food to the people who sold it, to the people who ate it. It's harder now to see those connections, let alone understand them!

So does that mean that we should stop buying so much stuff? Well, maybe. We should at least think about what we buy and how it affects the rest of our planet.

For instance, who made the clothes you are wearing right now? Were those people treated well while they worked? Did they receive fair wages? Did the factory that made your clothes release pollution into the environment?

These are all important questions to ask. And by asking them, you can help us all realize what is most important.

Money isn't evil. In fact, money gives us many wonderful opportunities. But money all alone isn't really all that valuable. After all, people are always more important than dollars. And none of us will have any wealth in the long run if we destroy our planet.

As the saying goes, you can't buy happiness! That's something you have to create for yourself, by using money wisely.

Other Perspectives on Wealth: COMMUNISM AND SOCIALISM

Capitalism is not the only economic system. Many of the world's nations have experimented with other systems, including communism and socialism. Karl Marx, the gentleman shown on the next page, is often referred to as the Father of Socialism.

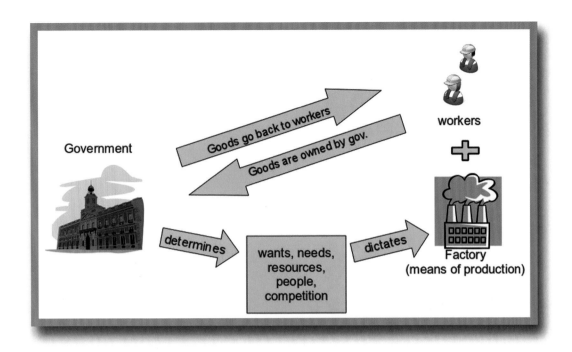

Socialists believe that the goverment should get involved with the economy. Instead of **free enterprise**, they believe that the economy should be carefully planned, so that resources (and money) are spread out more equally.

Communism takes it a step further. In communist nations, there is no private property; the government owns everything. Ideally, this should mean that no poverty or injustice exists. In real life, communism hasn't had a very good success rate. The governments that practiced it (like the Soviet Union) ended up oppressing their citizens.

OTHER CULTURAL PERSPECTIVES ON WEALTH

Capitalism, socialism, and communism have been the main economic systems in the modern world. But a few places and societies have tried out simpler alternatives.

For instance, before the coming of white people, the native people of Hawaii and much of North America had cooperative economies. This meant that each member of the community contributed to the entire community—and all benefited equally.

A few modern-day societies have tried to reproduce this simpler form of economy. The people who built the kibbutzim in Israel, the cooperative farms shown below, were trying to establish a new way of creating and sharing wealth, where everyone was equal and all shared in both the work and the profits. The kibbutzim were originally small farming communities that eventually grew to include some industries as well. Rather than being run by the government of Israel, they functioned within the rest of Israel, as an alternative to capitalism.

In the United States, during the 1960s and '70s, some people also tried to build small cooperative communes. Modern-day life is so complicated, however, that many people decided that living an alternative lifestyle is just too hard and takes too much work!

A World Without Money?

Have you ever watched a science fiction movie or television show where money no longer exists?

Some people wonder if maybe one day human beings will grow beyond the need for money. They dream of the day when humanity will become wise enough to create governments that don't oppress their citizens, worlds where everyone cooperates for the common good, the way they did in simpler or more primitive societies. In those future worlds, poverty and inequality and oppression will no longer exist. Everyone will be truly equals, with the same opportunities for all. Wars will no longer be fought over wealth, and crimes will no longer be committed for money. Everyone will have exactly what they need.

Other science fiction writers, however, look toward the future and picture a far different scenario. They believe that selfishness will always be a part of human nature—and without some economic system to govern human selfishness (whether capitalism or social-ism or communism), human greed would run rampant. There will always need to be some form of money, according to this perspective, because that's the only way to keep things fair.

What Do You Think?

Money is an important topic. It's not just dollars and cents, and learning to balance your checkbook. Thinking about money has to do with deciding what it is you truly value most. It also has to do with politics and culture, even with religion. People feel strongly about these topics, but that doesn't mean there are always right or wrong answers.

As you grow older, you will need to make up your own mind about what's most important to you. Here are some questions for you to consider:

- What is worth more—a friendship or a car?

- What would you be willing to spend more money for—a new medicine that would cure thousands of people, or a new technology that would produce more cars?

- Should governments ever get involved with the economy? Why or why not? Or in some ways but not others?

- How important is money to you? Can you imagine living without it?

- How can you help build a world where there is more wealth for everyone— or does freedom mean that it's up to the individual to take care of herself?

- Can you imagine a world where all money is electronic? What do you think the hardest thing would be about a world like that?

- Do you think the day will come when people will no longer use money? Why or why not?

- What's YOUR definition of wealth? And how does it connect to money?

These are important questions—but remember, it's up to you to decide the right answers!

Here's What You Need to Remember

- Money symbolizes everything that people value. It can be traded for other things that people value an equal amount. In our lives today, this has replaced bartering for different goods and services.

- Paper money was originally I.O.U. notes to other people, and these banknotes became official when people realized paper was a lot easier to carry around than a bunch of coins! Today, a lot of the money we deal with isn't in currency form. Instead, we wire things electronically, using computers.

- Paper bills represent the money a government has. If more bills are printed than money, inflation occurs and the paper money loses most of its value—like what happened in the South during the American Civil War.

- The economy is the distribution of goods and services within a country. This is understood by measuring the GDP, or the measure of everything produced in a country.

- There are many systems that countries can use to run their economies, including capitalism, communism, and socialism. The United States is a capitalist country.

Words You Need to Know

circulating: Passing from person to person or place to place.

currency: Money; something used to exchange for goods or services.

cyber: Relating to computers or the Internet.

demand: The amount of something wanted at a certain time.

denominations: Different values or sizes of money.

electronic: Relating to how information is spread with the use of electricity and machines; for example, through computers and televisions.

free enterprise: The right of private businesses to run their operations as they like, without government control.

laundering: To transfer illegal money to somewhere else to hide where it came from and make it look legal.

medieval: Relating to the Middle Ages, or the period of history between 600–1600.

mint: A place where money is made.

philosophy: Ideas that affect how people act and what they believe.

redeemed: Traded in for something of value.

reputable: Trustworthy or well-thought of.

standard: Something considered the rule for the measure of something. For example, the pound is a standard; it always weighs exactly the same amount no matter what is being weighed.

statistic: Something that deals with the interpretation of the actions or identities of lots of different groups of things. For example, to say that one out of every two people is a girl is a statistic.

supply and demand: The idea that the price of goods won't go above what people are willing to pay, but the demand for the goods won't allow the price to go down that much either.

tender: Something that may be offered as payment, such as money.

transactions: Exchanges of money, goods, and services.

FURTHER READING

Ferguson, Niall. *The Ascent of Money: A Financial History of the World.* New York: The Penguin Press, 2008.

Galbraith, John Kenneth. *Money: Whence It Came, Where It Went.* Boston, Mass.: Houghton Mifflin, 2001.

Karlitz, Gail. *Growing Money: A Complete Investing Guide for Kids.* New York: Price Stearn Sloan, 2001.

Maestro, Betsy and Giulio. *The Story of Money.* New York: Clarion Books, 1993.

FIND OUT MORE ON THE INTERNET

"Business and Money"
Howstuffworks
money.howstuffworks.com

"Fun Facts About Money"
Federal Reserve Bank of San Francico
www.frbsf.org/federalreserve/money/funfacts.html

Money News
USA Today
www.usatoday.com/money/default.htm

The websites listed on this page were active at the time of publication. The publisher is not responsible for websites that have changed their address or discontinued operation since the date of publication. The publisher will review and update the websites upon each reprint.

INDEX

Picture Credits

Al-Shukaili, Ahmed pp. 26–27

Bricktop; Creative Commons pp. 12–13

Castelazo, Tomas; Creative Commons pp. 10–11

Chic Design pp. 26–27

Clix pp. 52–53

de Florie, Trine pp. 8–9

Garrido I Puig, Marc pp. 14–15

Government of Israel pp. 50–51

Iker pp. 36–37

Kilian, Zsuzsanna pp. 40–41

Kragan, R; Creative Commons pp. 44–45

Lau, Enoch; Creative Commons pp. 14–15

Lopez, Jay pp. 32–33

Nowicki, W.; Creative Commons pp. 50–51

Patterson, Anita pp. 16–17

Prankster; Creative Commons pp. 12–13

Shutterman pp. 8–9

Simmonds, Dan pp. 8–9

Szczepanski, Przemyslaw pp. 24–25

Ram, Arte pp. 54–55

Relajp pp. 22–23

U.S. Navy pp. 46–47

Willis, Vaughan pp. 30–31

about the author and consultant

Rae Simons is a well-established educational author, who has written on a variety of topics for young adults for the past twenty years. She has also worked with financial advisors to produce adult-level books on money management.

Brigitte Madrian is Professor of Public Policy and Corporate Management in the Aetna Chair at Harvard University's Kennedy School of Government. She has also been on the faculty at the Wharton School and the University of Chicago. She is also a Research Associate at the National Bureau of Economic Research and coeditor of the *Journal of Human Resources*. She is the first-place recipient of the National Academy of Social Insurance Dissertation Prize and the TIAA-CREF Paul A. Samuelson Award for Scholarly Research on Lifelong Financial Security.